SEWING MASTERY

The Complete Beginner's Guide to Learn to Sew in Under 1 Day!

10 Step by Step Projects That Inspire You – Images Included

By Ellen Warren

© Copyright 2015

All rights reserved. No part of this book may be reproduced or transmitted in any form or by any means, electronically or mechanically, including photocopy, recording, or by and information storage or retrieval system, without the written permission from the publisher, except in the case of brief quotations embodied in critical articles or reviews.

Trademarks are the property of their respective holders. When used, trademarks are for the benefit of the trademark owner only.

DISCLAIMER

The information provided herein is stated to be truthful and consistent, in that any liability, in terms of inattention or otherwise, by any usage or abusage of any policies, processes, or directions contained within is the solitary and utter responsibility of the recipient reader. Under no circumstances will any legal responsibility or blame be held against the publisher for any reparation, damages, or monetary loss due to the information herein, either directly or indirectly. Respective authors hold all rights not held by publisher.

Note from the Author:

Welcome to the amazing world of Sewing! As some of you know from my other books, this has been a passion of mine for more than 15 years, and I'm thrilled that you will allow me to help you learn this beautiful art form. Sewing is such a part of our everyday life, that we take it for granted! This book for beginners is designed to give you an introduction to several different forms of sewing, both basic and more decorative. You'll learn basic hand stitching, what types of stitches your sewing machine can produce and when to use them, as well as some decorative sewing techniques like applique and embroidery.

Once you read this book, and complete the basic projects, you'll be well on your way to having both the skills and the confidence necessary to start trying your hand at a vast number of different sewing projects. Whether you want to sew for fun, help decorate your house, make yourself something new to wear, or hoping to start a new business, you'll be surprised at just how fast you can pick up this new handicraft.

Sewing is a unique blend of art and manual skills. You need to have the skill to make the designs and to be able to see the finished product through its completion, before you begin even making the cuts. At the same time, once you begin following a pattern, you may find that sewing is mainly a form of physical dexterity.

So whether you used to sew but fell out of the habit and are hoping to regain your lost skills, or you've never picked up a needle and thread before, after reading this book you will be well on your way to creating dozens of beautiful, handmade items.

Let's get started!!

Ellen Warren

Chapter Index

5

Introduction

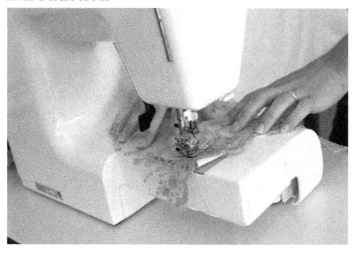

Sewing is one of those handicrafts that can take on numerous forms and variations. Sewing can be a livelihood, a craft, a hobby, a way that you make repairs. It can be a necessity, and it can also be something you do simply for enjoyment. It can also be an art form, and a way that you express yourself through the mediums of fabric and thread. For many people, sewing can also be considered a life skill, because you can use it to enhance your life in so many ways, whether through decorating your home or clothing your body.

Sewing was once taught in school as a skill that most 11 year olds needed to learn, but this has faded away as sewing fell out of favor as a life skill and became more of a hobby instead. While most women and girls once needed to know how to sew their own dresses for economy or merely because there wasn't enough selection, nearly everyone is able to pick up machine made clothing at even less than it will cost to make similar dresses from fabric bolts. This has left upcoming generations of people who have no idea how to do basic stitches that can help them tack up a hem that came undone, or to run up a new slipcover for a pillow that's become stained. And for those that did learn basic sewing at a young age, many of those same people only learned the very basic stitching needed for repair – not the more intricate and decorative types of sewing that can be used to enhance your clothing and home. This lack of knowledge means that while you may be inspired to try your hand at the many different types of sewing that are out there, you may not have the confidence in yourself that is required to take on a new hobby – especially one that requires at least some degree of skill.

This book for beginners is designed to give you an introduction to several different forms of sewing, both basic and more decorative. You'll learn basic hand stitching, what the types of stitches your sewing machine can produce and when to use them, as well as some decorative sewing techniques like applique and embroidery. This is intended to give you a thorough grounding in the world of sewing, boosting your skill and confidence levels enough that you'll feel encouraged by your results and ready to take on the next big thing that comes along.

Whenever you take up a new hobby that has so many different facets, like sewing, it's important to try them all at least once. You never know what exactly is going to catch your fancy, and which one you're going to get the hang of the quickest. Therefore, even if you just want to learn some basic sewing stitches, you may still want to take the time to complete a cross-stitch sampler, or to applique something onto a shirt front. Sewing projects are so easy once you learn the basic stitches that you'll have no trouble finding all kinds of fun things to do once you've begun. For example, your basic sewing machine only has two stitches with some variations thrown in for size and spacing. But a basic sewing machine can produce a wide range of different items, both decorative and utilitarian. Hand sewing is the same way, which is why it can be so important to try so many different types and variations before you decide to really become proficient in just one.

At the end of this book, you'll find instructions for 10 simple sewing projects from crafts to clothing so that you can try out your new skills for yourself. Once you've given them a try, you'll be in a good place to begin branching out into a variety of other sewing types and projects all your own. You'll also have a sense of how to sew without using a paper pattern, so you can feel free to begin designing things that you dream up, rather than just settling for things that someone else has already created.

Sewing can be fun, rewarding, and easy once you get going. So let's start examining the many reasons why you may want to try taking up this ancient handicraft.

Chapter 1: Reasons to Take Up Sewing

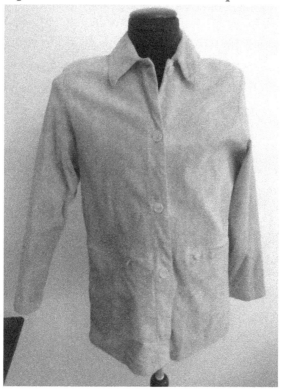

Like many of today's handicrafts, sewing began as something of a skill or a necessity, but eventually became something that people did for fun or as a hobby. Sewing dates all the way back to the ancient Egyptians where layers of cloth were stitched together with a needle and thread for a variety of purposes. This makes sewing one of the longest lasting – and one of the most basic – skill sets around. For someone that has never sewn before, however, the entire process can be a little intimidating. After all, when you see the kinds of projects people are turning out on Pinterest, you can often feel defeated before you've even begun, comparing your skills to the skills of the people turning out these amazing and beautiful projects.

There are a lot of reasons why you may want to consider taking up sewing, however, regardless of what you want to do with your finished results. Beyond having the skills necessary to complete any kind of project that catches your eye, you can also:

- Improve your hand eye coordination
- Learn to blend color and make art or decorations with a very different medium
- Copy expensive or designer clothes or costumes for less money
- Start a small side business making crafts, bags, clothes, or accessories
- Express yourself through fabric
- Have something to do with your hands during down time

- Learn a relaxing skill that keeps your hands busy while your mind is free

Best of all, you'll be learning a new skill that can challenge you and give you a great sense of accomplishment. After all, there's nothing quite like finishing a project like a new skirt, and trying it on for the first time, or completing a new set of curtains or a new slipcover that can transform a room of your home in just minutes.

Sewing may no longer be taught as a life skill, but it is an important to one to have in your repertoire. Over the years, sewing has enabled me to decorate my home, turn my child's baby clothes into a cherished heirloom, alter pants that my kids' have outgrown into shorts they can get another summer out of, and more. Best of all, with so many different types of sewing out there, you don't have to be an artist or a creative type to enjoy the benefits of learning to sew. All you have to have is a willingness to try new things, and a flair for the creative to help you visualize your projects through to the end right from the beginning.

Chapter 2: Types of Sewing

One of the reasons that sewing is such a broad type of hobby to learn, is that there are so many different kinds. And many of these types have subcategories that can branch out in seemingly endless ways, such as the many different kinds of cross stitch, or the multiple types of embroidery stitches that you can learn.

This basic overview of sewing types will help you get an understanding for what they are, as well as for when you may want to use them.

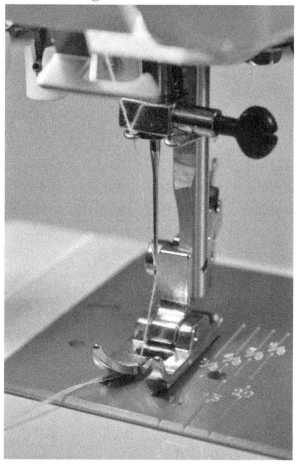

Sewing by machine is a lot faster than attempting the same project by hand, which is why so many people want to learn how to use a sewing machine, and figure out what it can do. Your basic sewing machine has a lot of functions. It can:

- Sew straight or curved lines with stitches of varying lengths
- Make zig-zag stitches of different sizes and length
- Make loose basting-style stitches that can hold things together temporarily while you put in more decorative stitching later

Depending on your machine, you may also be able to make decorative top stitching and embroidery as well. And while a standard sewing machine doesn't seem as though it has that many functions, you can use those few functions in a variety of ways to get the finished piece you're after.

For example, a sewing machine can:

- Sew two pieces of fabric together near the edge to form a hem
- Piece together several smaller sections of fabric, such as a quilt block
- Zig-zag stitch the raw edges of fabric to help prevent them from fraying over time
- Applique thin pieces of fabric onto another section of fabric by either straight sewing or zig-zag stitching the edges

And when you stop to think about all the many projects that just quickly stitching multiple pieces of fabric together can make, your sewing machine can quickly become your best friend.

Hand Sewing

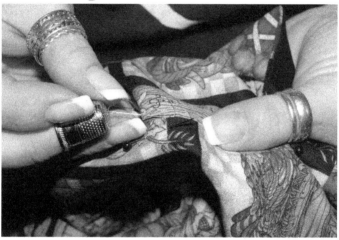

Even if you decide that you want to make the majority of your projects by machine, you should still learn a few basic stitches by hand. Why? Some projects may need you to finish a small section by hand, or you may find yourself far from home with a hem that's suddenly fallen and no machine to help tack it up. You can also stitch by hand anywhere, from the office, school, the park – bringing along your sewing machine is a lot more awkward and cumbersome than just bringing a needle and some thread.

Stitching by hand also gives you a lot more options than your machine does. Remember, unless you've purchased a fancy machine that can do embroidery and decorative stitching, you're only going to get things like that if you stitch them up by hand.

Using basic hand stitches you can:

- Sew a hem
- Tack up a hem to machine sew later
- Piece together multiple pieces of small fabric, such as a quilt block
- Blanket stitch two edges together such as craft felt to make a unique design or applique
- Make decorative applique stitches using embroidery thread
- Embroider names, designs, and varying colors into clothing
- Cross stitch a design for display or for use on clothing

And this is just the start. Machines make things easy and fast to put together, but they have limitations. Hand stitching lets you make all the same things, plus multiple others with a lot of different decorative stitches at the same time. So when you're learning how to sew, you should take the time to learn at least a few different types of hand stitching at the same time, so you can expand your productivity later.

Embroidery

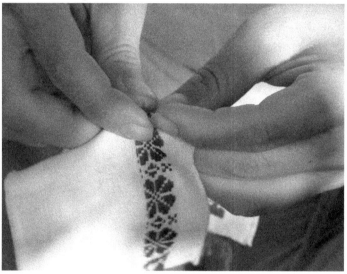

If you want to put your own personal stamp on anything from tablecloths to clothes, embroidery is the way to do it. Embroidery involves making decorative, colorful patterns and images on cloth using a special heavy thread and various types of stitches. Most embroidery involves a variety of different stitches and colors within a pattern. You can use any type of cloth to embroider, and you can also embroider using some specialty sewing machines.

Embroidery can be a fun way to sew your name onto something, stitch the outline of a car onto a toddler's t-shirt, or to make a 3-D raised design around the collar of a shirt. Once you've learned some basic hand sewing stitches, it's easy to make the jump to embroidery by using some of the same stitches as your starting point and placing them where they can be seen, with a thread and needle large enough to give you the look you're after.

Cross-Stitching

Cross stitching can also be used to decorate fabric, but it differs from embroidery in a few ways. There are several different cross-stitches, but the basic principle remains the same; you make two stitches per square of fabric, with the two stitches crossing or intersecting with one another in some way.

To achieve this, cross stitching is usually done on fabric that is easily divided into a grid, such as linen. Cross-stitched patterns can take on many different looks, from abstract color to detailed scenes, but they all have a similar geo-metric look to them based on the grid of the fabric and the nature of the stitches.

Cross-stitching is fairly simple once you get the hang of it, and it can be a relaxing way to add some color and detail to your life. The repetitive nature of the stitches means that you don't have to pay close attention to what you are doing, much like knitting, which makes cross-stitching a great activity for when you're watching TV or waiting for an appointment.

Applique

Applique is the process of layering pieces of fabric into a pattern. This could be cutting out shapes and attaching them to a shirt, or it could be attaching a decorative border to a set of curtains.

There are a number of ways you can applique. The most common involves simply stitching around the edge of a shape to attach it to the one below. Depending on what type of fabric you're using, however, this may not be enough, because the fabric edge could either curl or unravel. To fix this, you can either fold the edge of the decorative piece under before stitching it done, or you could can use a

22

different type of stitch to help cover the edge of the decorative piece to hold it flat and prevent any unraveling.

Any type of fabric can be used in applique. Felt, jersey knit, cotton; you can get very creative with the applique process joining together multiple shapes and colors. I once appliqued a felt bus onto my son's shirt using embroidery thread and a blanket stitch.

Using applique can let you decorate and personalize nearly anything. And because you can use simple stitches or even a sewing machine to do so, anyone can learn to applique no matter what your level of expertise with a needle and thread.

Chapter 3: Basic Sewing Stitches

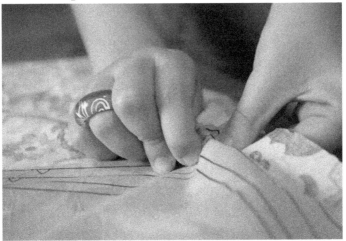

Sewing stitches are so numerous it's nearly impossible to list and catalogue them all together. Most people, however, will find that just mastering a few of each type will give you all the skill you need to complete a wide number of different projects. Once you've learned these stitches, you can always go on to learn other, more decorative types once you get involved in a specific project or sewing type.

Basting

Basting is one of the easiest and most simple types of sewing. It's meant to temporarily join two pieces of fabric together so you can go back later and permanently stitch them together. Basting is fast and can be done on the fly as well. If, for example, the hem of your skirt falls down at work, you can quickly baste it back into place, then fix it once you get home. Basting is used when you don't have pins to hold things together, and it is also used when making a quilt to hold your layers together before putting in the quilting stitches.

To baste:

1. Gather up any size needle and thread.
2. Thread the needle and knot the ends of the thread together.
3. Place your two pieces of fabric together where they need to be joined.
4. Push your needle through both pieces of fabric up from the bottom or underside so your knot doesn't show, and pull the thread taut.
5. Move down the fabric anywhere from 1/8-inch to 1-inch depending on how large you want your stitches to be and push the needle back through to the underside.
6. Move the needle along the fabric about as much as you did for your first stitch, so if you used a 1-inch stitch, you'll move it along 1-inch on the underside, and push it back up to the

top, trying to keep your stitches in a straight line.

7. Go forward another set amount and go back to the underside again.

8. Continue until you reach the end of the fabric.

The basting stitch when finished will have evenly sized stitches and gaps moving along the fabric in a row. This will securely hold the fabric in place until you can make a more permanent stitch. The larger the stitches you make, the faster you'll go, but the less secure this will be. For example, if you're tacking up a hem, you may want to use smaller stitches to ensure it holds to the end of the day without snagging, but if you're quilting, you can use larger stitches because there will be so many of them, along with a quilting frame to hold everything in place.

Back Stitching

If you've ever examined a hem that's been done on a sewing machine, you're seeing an example of a back stitch, or a row of stitches that are all connected to one another with no spaces between them.

Back stitching is a more secure, permanent way to join to pieces of fabric together or to make a hem. Like basting, you can make your stitches larger or smaller depending on how quickly you want to work, and how long you need this stitch to last. The smaller the stitches, the less they will show, and the longer they will hold – decades instead of years, for example. You can use any size of needle or thread to back stitch, but the smaller the needle, the smaller your stitches will be, and the easier time you'll have going through thick fabrics.

To back stitch:

1. Thread your needle and tie off the ends.
2. Position the pieces of cloth you intend to stitch. You may want to use pins or a basting stitch to hold them while you work because you'll be moving a lot more slowly, and you don't want your fabric to slip.
3. Make a guide you can follow with your stitches to help keep them straight with a chalk or fabric pencil and a ruler. You'll stitch right on this mark so your finished stitch line will be even. Once you're done, wash the fabric and the mark will come out.
4. Push your needle and thread up through the back of the fabric where the knot will not show. Pull the thread taut.
5. Make a single stitch in the direction you want your row of stitches to go and push the needle and thread back to the underside of the fabric.

This first stitch should ideally be the size you want your finished stitches to be.

6. Pull your thread taut on the underside of the fabric and move your needle down your mark about as far as your first stitch was. Push the needle up from the back and pull it tight. There will now be a small gap between your first stitch and where you thread is now.

7. Move your needle back to the end of the first stitch and push it back down to the underside at the same point where the first stitch ends. This will produce your second stitch, which will be connected to your first stitch.

8. Repeat until you reach the end of the guide. This will give you a chain of connected stitches that will securely hold your fabric.

Keep in mind that the back stitch only produces a row of neat stitches on the top of the fabric. The underside will have longer, less connected stitches that aren't as neat or nice to look at. For this reason, only use the back stitch on items where the top is the only thing that shows.

Whip Stitch

The whip stitch is another very fast stitch. It's typically used to close edges, such as an opening on a pillow or to attach a hem without extremely visible stitches, such as in knit fabrics. It's a stronger, longer-lasting stitch than basting produces, so it's good for those times when you need to work quickly, but need your work to hold.

The whip stitch is a round stitch, meaning that it produces a circular motion as you sew. If you're sewing two ends together, the stitch will be visible in a row of circular stitches across the top. If you're tacking up a hem, you'll see a row of vertical stitches on the back of the fabric, but only a tiny stitch every so often on the front.

To make the whip stitch:

1. Thread your needle and knot the ends of the thread.
2. Pin the edges of your fabric together where you want the stiches to be, leaving one end slightly open.
3. Start your first stitch between the two layers of fabric, pushing your needle from the middle to the back. This will hide your knot between the two layers, since the whip stitch is often a visible one.
4. Pull your thread taut on the back of the fabric, then pull it up toward the top of the two pieces you are joining.

5. Wrap the thread over the top and push the needle back down right next to the first stitch, rather than right on top of it. Your finished stitches will go at a slight angle rather than straight up and down.
6. Repeat until you've completely joined the two pieces of fabric.

Like with the other stitches, you can vary your spacing between them, but the closer you can stitch, the tighter you'll hold the fabric together. If both sides of your fabric will be visible, try to keep the place where the thread goes in and out even. You can use a line drawn on the fabric if necessary to make your stitches even.

Basic Cross Stitch

While embroidery and cross stitching are very different forms of sewing, you may want to start with cross stitching before you move on to embroidery. Because of the way that cross-stitch projects follow a grid, you can more easily map out your design and get used to the larger needle and higher thread count than with a more freehand embroidery project.

When you start cross stitching, you may want to begin with a special type of cloth called aida. Aida is an inexpensive cloth that has a very pronounced grid. It's easier to use than linen, which makes it ideal for your first projects. Once you begin to get the hang of it, and you want to make something more ambitious, you can easily switch over to linen.

Unlike most other forms of sewing, cross stitching requires additional tools beyond a needle and thread. Part of the process of cross stitching means that the fabric needs to be pulled very taut as you push the needle through. To achieve this, you'll need to get a fabric hoop.

The fabric hoop is made up of two circles, often made of wood or metal. You'll put the fabric over the inner hoop, and tighten the outer hoop around the edges. This will pull your fabric tight in the center, and give you a very firm surface to stitch on.

Hoops come in all sizes. If you use a small one, you'll just need to reposition your fabric a few times over the course of the project. Large ones are easier to work bigger sections of the design, but they can be a little cumbersome to hold.

Both cross stitching and embroidery will use the same needles and a heavier thread known as floss. Embroidery floss comes in a skein of six threads twisted together to form one heavier thread. You can stitch with anywhere from one to six threads at a time, depending on how heavy you want the finished stitches to be. Some projects will specify the size of the needle and the number of threads, as well as the exact colors.

Most floss comes with a color number; you'll use this number to find the right colors for your project.

To make a basic cross stitch:

1. Thread your embroidery needle with the requisite number of threads and knot off the ends.
2. Stretch a piece of fabric tightly between your hoops with the area you want to work toward the center.
3. Locate the square you want to begin working in, and find one corner of it from below.
4. Push your needle up from below on your selected corner and pull your thread taut.
5. Push your needle down again on the opposite diagonal corner on the same square. This will make a line cutting across the square so the square will now resemble two triangles.
6. Push your needle up from the bottom again on one of the empty corners of the same square. Pull your thread taut.

7. Cross your initial stitch to go to the opposite diagonal corner to push your needle down again. Pull your thread taut.

This produces the basic X cross stitch. You can continue to make X's across the area with the same color, or vary your color per square to change the pattern. It is not uncommon for a person to have multiple needles threaded with different colors so you can work a complex pattern quickly to get the design you want.

Basic Embroidery

In a lot of ways embroidery and cross stitching have a lot in common. The differences lie in:

- The fabric
- The variety of stitches

Embroidery can be done on aida or linen, but it can also be carried out on other fabrics as well. This is primarily because you don't need to have a grid. You can embroider in more flowing shapes and with different sizes of stitches that aren't dependent on things like overlapping threads.

You can embroider using a very simple back stitch, as well as more decorative stitches. When you're first starting out, your challenges will be mostly with the larger needle and thread, as well as changing the direction of your stitches and blending colors. Once you get the hang of these, you can start to branch out to different stitches.

One way you can get used to embroidering, is to trace something simple onto the fabric with a marker or pen. This can be a name, or a flower and vine. Then perform a simple back stitch along your traced lines using different colors as you go. You'd be surprised at home many shapes you can make using this stitch, including things like flower petals. The trick with embroidery lies in the colors; consider trying some variegated thread to give your early work more dimension as you get used to blending colors.

Basic Applique

Applique is a little different than other types of sewing because it's the process of layering one fabric on top of another and joining them around the top layer's edge. You can use any stitch that you want to do this, including basic back stitching, blanket stitching, whip stitching, or using a machine. This will all depend on what you want the finished piece to look like, and what type of fabric you're using. For example, something that unravels may need a stitch or technique that covers the edges, while something heavy like felt can have the edges left alone.

The basic applique process doesn't change too much beyond the stitching, however. To do some very simple applique:

1. Trace and cut out the shape you want to applique onto your other fabric.
2. Line up where you want the shape to go and pin it into place. If your fabric will unravel or you don't want an edge showing, fold the edge under about ¼-inch and pin it here. You'll stitch through the fold so you'll have a finished edge with no raw fabric showing.
3. Thread your needle and push it up from below to start your first stitch.
4. Stitch around your shape as close to the edge as you can get. You can back stitch or whip stitch for your first time, or machine stitch until you get used to the process. After this, you can try some decorative stitches on top of the applique to help give the finished piece a distinctive look.

Chapter 4: Projects for Beginners

Whether you've mastered your basic stitches and are looking for something a little more challenging, or you're just looking to boost your confidence by completing a few simple designs before moving on to something else, these projects are designed to help you get to where you're going. By completing each project from start to finish, you'll be tackling a lot of small problems that will ensure you're gaining the skills necessary to take on something bigger down the road.

Project 1: Making a Pillow

Making a pillow is one of the first projects any beginner should take on. This project combines measuring, cutting, pinning, machine sewing, and hand sewing to complete. You can use your choice of fabrics and colors, and you can also adjust the size if desired to make pillows for any room of your home.

What you'll need:

- ½ yard of fabric in your choice
- Ruler or measuring tape
- Washable fabric pen
- Scissors or rotary cutter and mat
- Pins
- Sewing machine
- Needle and thread
- Soft fill

What you'll do:

1. Fold your fabric in half and cut on the fold. This will give you to pieces of fabric of the same size to work from.
2. Measure your fabric and mark out 15-1/4 inches in each direction so you form a square on each piece. To make this easier, you can stack your fabric on top of itself and pin it together before cutting out your squares. When you are done, you should have two 15-1/2-inch squares of fabric.
3. Turn your fabric inside out and pin the edges together on three sides about ¼-inch in around all the edges.
4. Use your sewing machine to sew up the edges of the pillow ¼-inch in all the way around on the three sides.

5. Measure in 5-inches on either side of the open end of the fabric. Pin the fabric edges together ¼-inches in, up to the 5-inch mark. This will leave an opening in the center of the fourth side.
6. Sew the ends where pinned up to the opening.
7. Turn your pillow right side out through the opening.
8. Stuff your pillow with soft fill until it is as firm as you would like.
9. Turn your pillow on its end so that the opening faces up.
10. Carefully fold the edges of the opening in toward each other and pinch the opening shut.
11. Pin along the ¼-inch mark to hold the opening closed.
12. Thread your needle and start your first stitch between the two layers of the opening.
13. Whip stitch across the opening to close it up.
14. Admire your new pillow.

Project 2: Making Curtains

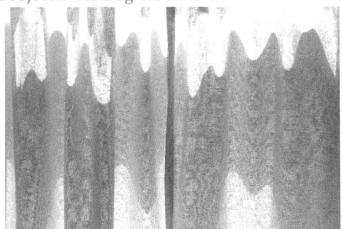

Making a set of curtains for your windows is incredibly easy, and can usually be completed in under an hour. This is a great way of bring some new color and detail to any room, and at a fraction of the price of purchasing similar curtains from the store.

What you'll need:

- Measuring tape
- Fabric of your choice
- Scissors or rotary cutter and mat
- Pins
- Sewing machine

What you'll do:

1. Measure your window. This is tricky, because what you want to do is measure where the curtain will fall, not the window frame itself. For example, your curtain rod will likely be installed a few inches above your window, and extend out a few inches on either side. Likewise, you'll want your curtains to extend past the bottom of your window by a few inches at a minimum as well. So you may want to measure out approximately 4-inches all the way around your window frame. Now divide this measurement in half vertically; this is how large each of your curtain panels will need to be.

2. Purchase the requisite amount of fabric. Any fabric can be used for curtains from burlap to lace; just be sure you determine if you want your curtains to block light and use the appropriate fabric.

3. Measure out your curtain panels, plus 2-inches on each side. This is to give you a nice thick hem and a pocket for your rod at the top. Cut out your panels.

4. Measure 2-inches in on each side and fold your fabric on this mark. Pin your fabric down to make your hems and pocket. Keep in mind that

you will need to leave the ends open on either side of your pocket to insert the rod. The way to do this is to hem the sides of the curtain first, the hem the top and bottom, which will give you a built in pocket with finished edges.

5. Sew straight lines along each hem starting with the two sides, then the bottom, and finally the top.
6. Slide your rod through the pocket at the top of each panel and hang your new curtains.

Project 3: Appliqueing with a Blanket Stitch

The blanket stitch is a fun edge stitch that is worth learning for a variety of reasons. You can use it applique thick shapes, join to pieces of fabric together

42

on the edges, or finish a blanket. You'll use embroidery thread and a large needle for this project, and you may want to consider using felt for your first project, as felt does not unravel or require you to pin it under on the edges.

What you'll need:

- T-shirt
- Felt
- Scissors
- Pins
- Embroidery needle and thread

What you'll do:

1. Cut a basic shape out of your felt. You can use two or three colors of felt to make multiple pieces of one larger design if you desire; you'll applique each piece separately onto the t-shirt.
2. Line up the felt shape or shapes on the t-shirt where desired. Pin them into place to hold them while you stitch.
3. Thread your embroidery needle. You'll want to use roughly three strands of thread so that the stitch will show. Remember that you are doubling your thread when you put it through the needle, so three strands will give you a six strand stitch.

4. Go inside the t-shirt with your needle and push it up through the t and felt from below about 1/8-inch from the edge of the felt. Pull your thread taut.

5. Move your thread over slightly as if you were going to whip stitch and push the needle back down into the t-shirt just past the felt. Do not pull your thread taut, and leave a small loop instead.

6. Push your needle back up through the felt and t-shirt together again. This time, push your needle under the small loop you left before, then pull your thread taut. This will grab the thread and leave a vertical stitch and a horizontal stitch along the top of the felt.

7. Repeat this stitch all the way around the shape to completely applique it onto the shirt.

Project 4: Appliqueing with a Machine

Appliqueing with a machine is very simple and easy to do. You can use any type of fabric, including thin cottons that might be difficult to stitch by hand without unraveling. This technique is also super-fast and you can turn out multiple designs in a short period of time.

What you'll need:

- T-shirt
- Fabric of your choice
- Scissors
- Pins

- Sewing machine

What you'll do:

1. Cut out your shape in the fabric of your choice. When you cut, measure out ¼-inch from what you want the finished size of the shape to be and cut along this line. This will enlarge your shape ¼-inch all the way around.
2. Take a look at your shape. Anywhere that it changes direction, like a corner, make a cut into the corner ¼-inch in. If you are using a circular shape, then make a slit every inch or so into the fabric. These slits will enable you to fold the edges under neatly without the fabric puckering.
3. Place your shape on the t-shirt where desired.
4. Fold the edges underneath the shape ¼-inch in and pin them securely into place on the shirt.
5. Open up your t-shirt and slide it onto the bottom of your machine so that the back of the shirt goes beneath the machine and only the area to be stitched is beneath the needle.
6. Line up your needle with the shape and stitch around the edge of the shape, removing pins as you go.
7. Cut your threads and remove the finished shirt from the machine.

Project 5: Making a Basic A-Line Skirt

There is nothing easier than making a basic A-line skirt out of knit jersey material. You don't need a pattern, just a measuring tape and some scissors, and you can alter the overall length and width of the skirt as often as you would like to change up the basic design. If you have an A-line skirt already in your closet, you can take it out to examine as you work, but that isn't necessary and you can make this skirt even without a visual model.

What you'll need:

- Measuring tape
- Knit jersey material
- Washable fabric marker or pen
- Scissors or rotary cutter and mat
- Pins
- Sewing machine

What you'll do:

1. Measure your waist where you'll want the skirt to fall. Don't add any extra as a seam allowance; jersey stretches and the seam allowance will help the skirt stay put once it's on you.
2. Measure from your waist down to where you want the skirt to end. To this measurement, you will add 12-inches. This will give you a fold over waistband, and a seam allowance for the bottom hem.
3. Lay out your fabric so that it is folded in half.
4. Using a fabric marker, measure out and mark a section 12-inches tall and as wide as your waist.

From the bottom of this point, measure down to the point where you want the skit to end and make a mark.

5. Measure out 3-inches on either side from your waist measurement at the bottom of the skirt. An A-line is bigger at the bottom than at the top. Connect your top and bottom by drawing a line from the wide bottom up to the bottom edge of your waist band. Your fabric should have a shape drawn on it that looks a little like a triangle with a rectangle on top rather than a point.

6. Pin your two layers of fabric together so they won't slip and cut out two identical shapes.

7. Separate your pieces; you'll need to work on the tops and bottoms of each one separately, then join them together on the sides.

8. Fold down the large rectangle on the top of each section in half. Pin in place.

9. Fold up the bottom edge about ¼-inch and pin to form a hem. Keep in mind that jersey does try to roll, so you may need to give yourself a little more room to work that you ordinarily would.

10. Sew along these two lines and repeat for the other section.

11. Pin the two pieces together wrong sides out.

12. Sew straight lines right up the two sides joining the skirt together on either end.
13. Try on your new skirt. The waist band can be folded down again or left tall depending on your personal preference.

Project 6: Making a Cross Stitch Sampler

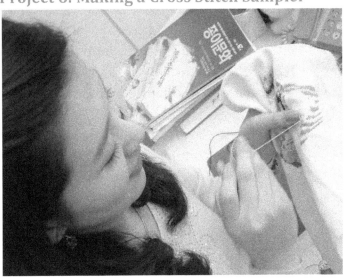

A sampler is a type of sewing done to showcase a "sample" of your work. In the case of cross stitching, this is usually a farmable square of fabric with a simple design worked into it. For the purpose of this project, you'll use the basic cross stitch outlined in Chapter 2. You can vary your colors if desired; the colors shown here are only a suggestion to let you work it out. Once you've completed this basic sampler, you can try your hand at more complicated patterns.

hat you'll need:

- Embroidery hoop
- Embroidery needle
- Four colors of embroidery floss
- Scissors
- Aida fabric

What you'll do:

1. Position your aida in the embroidery hoop and tighten it.
2. Count out squares so you'll know where to place your first stitches. You can make one or several of these simple trees to practice putting together several colors at once in a design.
3. Thread your needle with the first color. If desired, you can thread four needles with all four colors at once to make it easier to shift between them.
4. Make your first cross stich at the bottom of the pattern and work your way up until you need to change colors.

5. Continue counting squares and stitching until you complete the picture or pictures.

6. Remove the aida from the hoop.

Project 7: Joining Circles for a Craft Banner

You've probably come across these fun, decorative felt "banners" all over the internet at one point in time or another. Made up of circles, hearts, or other simple shapes, they can be found strung across windows, mantels, and walls to add some decorative or seasonal color to the home. Most people don't tend to mention how they made them, however, which can leave you wondering where they came from.

The answer is that they are made of two pieces of felt that have been blanket stitched together. The finalized circles or shapes are then strung and hung. They are incredibly easy to make, and you can create them in a wide variety of different color and shape combinations for any occasion.

What you'll need:

- Multiple sheets of felt in your desired colors
- Fabric marker with a fine tip
- Scissors
- Embroidery needle and floss
- String

What you'll do:

1. Trace the shape you want to string onto your banner onto your felt. You'll need two of each shape for one section. Prepare to trace a minimum of about 60 shapes, but you can always do more or less depending on the final size you want it to be.
2. Cut out the shapes, and take the time to match up sets of two.
3. Thread your needle with three strands of embroidery floss.
4. Pick up two shapes and insert the needle through one shape so that your knot is hidden in between them.
5. Go over the top of both shapes with your needle and push back through both shapes.

6. Push your needle under the thread that goes over the top and pull taut to complete your first stich. This is the blanket stitch; repeat it all the way around the shape, hiding your final knot in the center.
7. Repeat for all the matched shapes.
8. Put the end of a piece of string through the end of your needle and tie a knot very close to the eye. This will give you a long trailing end of string.
9. Thread your needle through each one of the shapes between the two layers, pushing them down the string as you go until you've put them all onto the string.
10. Slide the shapes down the string until they are evenly placed along it.
11. Hang your new banner.

Project 8: Making a Simple Bag

Making a bag sounds a lot more complicated than it actually is. While it's true that there are several bag patterns out there that are extremely difficult and time consuming to make, there are just as many bags that are so easy to put together, you don't even need a pattern to do so. This project is one of those; this bag was originally designed to hang from the back of a seat in the car to collect trash, but we've found countless other uses for it as well. Best of all, it takes only a few minutes to make, and you can alter the dimensions to get even more uses out of it. Once you've completed it, you may want to branch out with things like a lining and pockets to try making it your own.

What you'll need:

- Fabric of your choice – about a yard total – you may want a second fabric to act as the loop if desired
- Ruler or measuring tape
- Scissors or rotary cutter and mat
- Pins
- Sewing machine

What you'll do:

1. Lay out your fabric.
2. Measure out and mark two sections that measure 9-1/2-inches by 6-1/2-inches, two sections that measure 9-1/2-inches by 12-1/2-inches and one section that measures 12-1/2-inches by 6-1/2-inches.
3. Measure out and mark the handle at 6-inches wide by 24-inches long.
4. Cut out these sections.
5. Pin down about ¼-inch of fabric on top end of each section, so on one of the short sides of the thinner pieces of fabric, and on one of the long edges on the fatter pieces of fabric. This will form the finished edge on the bag.

6. Take the 12-1/2-inch by 6-1/2-inch section and one of the 9-1/2-inch by 6-1/2-inch sections. Pin them together on the short sides that have not been finished with the hem facing in and the right side of the fabric facing out. Repeat for the other side.
7. Sew up these two seams and remove the pins.
8. Take the 9-1/2-inch by 12-1/2-inch sections and pin them to the long edges of the bottom section and the long sides of the two side sections.
9. Turn the bag inside out and run up the seams. You will now have a pouch.
10. Take your piece of fabric for the strap and fold it in half lengthwise with the right sides of the fabric facing in, pinning the edges together.
11. Run a seam along this edge.
12. Turn the strap right side out.
13. Pin the two short ends of the strap to the inside edge of the bag on either of the short sides.
14. Sew the ends down securely.

You now have an open, pouch style bag. If you like, you can attach a snap to the center of the bag's top to close it.

Project 9: Make an Infinity Scarf

Infinity scarfs are all the rage right now. These versatile scarfs can be made out of any fabric or material from knit jersey to light chiffon. They are also incredibly easy to make, either by hand or by machine. In fact, they consist of only two straight seams, so you can whip up as many as you'd like in a very short amount of time. You can also vary the size, color, and material of the scarfs to form your own unique look.

What you'll need:

- Fabric of your choice
- Measuring tape
- Scissors or rotary cutter and mat
- Pins

- Sewing machine or needle and thread

What you'll do:

1. Lay out your fabric.
2. Measure out and mark 60-inches by 20-inches.
3. Cut out your fabric.
4. Fold the fabric in half lengthwise with the right sides facing in.
5. Pin the fabric together to hold it securely.
6. Sew along this line, either using the sewing machine or using a simple back stitch by hand. You will now have a long tube measuring 60-inches long by 10-inches wide.
7. Turn the tube right side out so that the seam is hidden on the inside.
8. Take one end of the fabric and fold the unfinished edges down so that they tuck inside of the tube. Pin them in place.
9. Take the other end of the fabric and fold the unfinished edges inside the tube.
10. Take the second end of the fabric and tuck it inside the other end of the tube. Pin everything together securely to hold it.
11. Sew a straight line across the tube where the two ends meet. You will now have a large circle of fabric that you can twist three times around your neck to form an infinity scarf.

Project 10: Make a Patchwork Doorstop Snake

Ever have trouble keeping a door open when the windows are also open allowing a breeze to blow through your home? Slamming doors can be startling at best and dangerous at worst, so many people choose to use some kind of doorstop to prevent this from happening. This easy sewing project will make you a door stop out of leftover pieces of fabric from other projects. Best of all, you can use this snake as a way to block drafts beneath a door in the wintertime, long after you no longer need it to help keep a door open in the nice weather.

Because this doorstop is filled with sand, you'll want to use a very tightly woven fabric. Things like linen or burlap will allow the finer particles of sand to pour out of the snack, getting all over your home. So be sure to use more tightly woven scraps. If you're in doubt, just wrap up a small amount of sand in a scrap of fabric and toss it in your hand a few times; if no dust appears to be leaking out, the fabric is find to use for this project.

What you'll need:

- At least 10 different scraps of material all measuring roughly 4-inches wide by 8-inches long – because this is a patchwork piece, it doesn't have to be perfectly even in width, just length
- Pins
- Sewing machine or needle and thread
- Bag of sand

What you'll do:

1. Lay out your fabric scraps side by side so you can see the placement of the colors. You can choose to lay out your fabrics randomly, or to make an alternating pattern of colors. If you choose, you can also make your swatches much thinner and use more of them or use swatches

of varying widths to change up the look and feel of the finished doorstop.

2. Turn your fabric swatches over once you've figured out the placement of the fabrics.

3. Pin the pieces together along their long edges so the seams are facing up and the right side of the fabric faces down. You should have a long joined section of fabric pinned together when you are done.

4. Run up each one of the seams on your sewing machine, or back stitch by hand along each one of the seams.

5. Fold the patchwork fabric in half lengthwise with the right sides of the fabric facing in.

6. Pin the two edges together.

7. Stitch up this long seam from one end to the next either by sewing machine or by hand.

8. Pin and stitch up one of the two open short ends on the fabric as well. This will form what looks like a long, inside out fabric sock.

9. Turn the fabric right side out to form a long tube open on one end.

10. Carefully pour sand into the tube from the open end. This is where your stitches will be put to the test; if you missed a section of fabric or your stitches are too big, the sand may slip out. If this happens, just pour the sand back

out, turn the tube inside out again and redo the loose section.

11. Once the tube is filled with sand, tuck the edges of the open end of the tube in on themselves and pinch the opening together. Pin it securely shut.

12. Sew up the opening either using a straight stitch on the sewing machine going through the top of the fabric close to the mouth, or using a whip stitch by hand over the mouth of the opening.

13. Place your new doorstop by your door to hold it open and enjoy.

Conclusion

By now you'll hopefully be inspired to begin trying a few sewing projects of your own. Once you complete the basic projects outlined in this book, you'll be well on your way to having both the skills and the confidence necessary to start trying your hand a vast number of different sewing projects.

Whether you want to sew for fun, to help decorate your house, make yourself something new to wear, or you're hoping to start a new business, you'll be surprised at just how fast you can pick up this new handicraft.

Sewing is a unique blend of art and manual skill. You need to have the eye necessary to make the designs and to be able to see the finished product through to its completion before you begin even making the cuts. At the same time, once you begin following a pattern, you may find that sewing is mainly a form of physical dexterity.

So whether you used to sew but fell out of the habit and are hoping to regain your lost skills, or you've never picked up a needle and thread before, you're now on your way to creating dozens of beautiful, handmade items.

Start with the basic projects and techniques outlined here, then take a look around you. From items already in your home to inspiration you'll find in stores and the internet, you'll be sure to find some new ideas that you'll want to try your hand at.

So start sewing, and find out why this handicraft is one that will last for generations, even after it's no longer being considered a life skill.

Preview of "ONE DAY BEADING MASTERY" by Ellen Warren

Introduction - The Amazing world of Bead Making!!

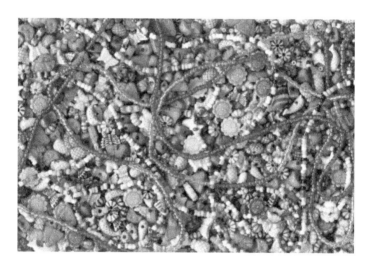

1 Photo by Piyachok Thawornmat

There are many different kinds of jewelry, but one of the richest and most complex types is made from beads. Beads and beaded jewelry can be found in nearly all cultures with many dating back hundreds to thousands of years. Beads can be made of clay, glass, stone, paper, wood, plastic, and metal. They can be found in hundreds of shades and colors, as well as countless shapes and sizes. They can be expensive or cost just pennies a piece, making them accessible for nearly anyone who wants to start creating their own jewelry.

Beading and creating beaded jewelry is a great way of expressing yourself, creating your own personal style, and exercising your creativity. Whether you create something simple or complex, the very art of choosing colors and materials, determining placement, and stringing the beads can unlock your inner artist and personal stylist.

There are a lot of different ways you can use beads to create jewelry. From wire wrapping to coralling, beads can be transformed into rings, bracelets, earrings, and necklace of any style, shape, or personal type of expression. These techniques can be used with beads of nearly any size and shape, from selecting a single color and size of bead to weaving together a variety of different beads made from a mixture of stone, glass, and shell.

So whether you're new to beads and creating beaded jewelry, or you've been experimenting with your own style for some time and are ready for more difficult techniques, learning to work with beads can be a fun and creative way to add some color, texture, and style to your life.

In this book you'll learn the basics of beading from selecting your materials to mixing colors and arranging your layout. You'll also learn some simple tricks for making your own beads out of paper, wood, and clay, and some more intermediate beading techniques to start challenging yourself with.

Beading can be as simple or as complex as you want it to be, making it the ideal medium for people of all levels of artistic expression. Whether you intend to make jewelry for yourself, as a gift, or to start your own craft business, learning to bead can open up a world of different possibilities for you.

Types of Beading

There are a lot of different ways that beads have been used to create various forms of jewelry and decoration. Beads can be strung, woven, or sewed, and there are several different techniques to achieve a variety of different effects.

- The most common type of beadwork is known as threading. This is the act of stringing beads one at a time onto a single strand of thread, wire, or nylon. You can get a lot of different effects using this one simple technique either by varying the beads, varying the length of the thread, or by combining multiple threads together, twisting the strands, or layering them.
- Coralling is type of threading that uses beads to create multiple branches combing off of a single row of beads. Think of the way that a piece of coral may branch in different directions. So using coralling, you can creating a necklace with several small offshoots or a set of earrings that move in various ways.
- Stitching is one of the more elaborate and complicated methods of beading. There are several different stitches including ladder stitches, brick stitches, peyote stitches, and spiral stitches. Most stitching techniques rely on seed beads or other types of very small beads so you can weave them together to form things like flowers made entirely out of beads.
- Loom beading is a method of weaving threads or stitches through a set of beads to create a sheet of beads. Bags, tassels, and any kind of jewelry meant to drape on the wearer is using woven using this type of technique. Unlike

other types of beading, which don't need special equipment beyond the beads, thread, and possibly a needle, loom beading does require both a set pattern and a beading loom to create the desired effects.

Most people when setting out to start making beaded jewelry begin with threading. This technique is so simple that it allows you to work on things like color, texture, and design without worrying about the intricacies of stitches or the type of thread you are using at the same time. You may want to start working with beads in a variety of different patterns at first until you become comfortable with the various effects you can create. After a while, you can begin branching into different stitches to create intricate pendan0ts, broaches, and earrings.

Layouts and Planning

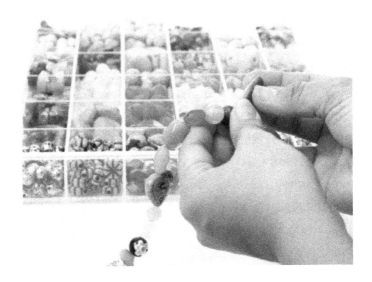

3 Photo by Stuart Miles

No matter what you plan on making, or what technique you'll eventually use, every design begins with the layout. This is the method of arranging your beads in the same order or pattern that you'll eventually use to create the finished piece of jewelry. When you're working with a lot of beads at once, it's helpful to plan while the beads are still loose.

Otherwise you can easily find yourself in a position of having a piece that isn't balanced, or that breaks pattern somewhere along the way. Your only recourse at this point in time is usually to start over, so a proper layout can save you a lot of time and frustration latter on.

Plastic trays are available that have narrow channels cut into them just for this purpose. It allows you to arrange your beads in the order you want them without worrying about them rolling away. You can adjust your tray size for the size of the piece that you're working on, and if you're creating a set pattern, you can start it in the tray to ensure that it will work for you before you start threading, without needing to lay out the entire thing.

Spacing

When you're taking the time to lay out your necklace, bracelet, or earrings, make sure you give some thought to the spacing of the beads at the same time. Spaces within a set of beads help the pattern come alive by giving the eye a chance to break apart of the larger sections. They aren't necessary; if you're creating a necklace made up of random beads or a bracelet made of all the same bead then spaces won't need to be part of the design. For other types of jewelry, however, spaces can add a lot of dimension and interest to the design.

Spaces can be achieved in your work in a few different ways:

- Using smaller, plain beads – sometimes known as spacers - between larger patterned ones to break them apart
- Using jump rings between beads to separate them and add dimension to the piece
- Using crimp beads along your wire or thread to stop a bead from sliding and leaving empty space on either side of a larger bead

Depending on the look you want to create, you should take the time to play around with the spacing. If you're using plain beads between patterned ones, consider using different sizes. You can also use varying sizes of the same bead to get similar effects.

Spacing is also a great way to get multiple looks out of one set of beads. For example, you could make a bracelet with patterned beads broken by plain beads of the same size. Then you could create a second bracelet using the same patterned beads broken by plain beads of a much smaller size. You could even go on to make a bracelet using the same patterned beads but with spaces left by links or empty spaces.

By playing around with these different looks during your layout, you can find the one that works best for the look that you're trying to achieve.

Color and Pattern

You will also want to take color and pattern into consideration when you plan your layout. Jewelry doesn't have to coordinate or even contain multiple shades of the same color, but may designs rely on a mixture of just two or three colors to get the desired look.

Some tips to help you blend things perfectly include:

- Pick up an accent color from within a patterned bead and select some plain beads in this color to intersperse. This will help break up the design and keep the patterned beads from overwhelming the piece.
- Introduce some neutral colors like white, black, gray, or brown to your piece. For example, if the jewelry you are working on seems too dark or looks all of the same color, adding some white can lighten it up dramatically. Likewise, using brown or black in a lighter colored piece can add gravity and interest to the design.

- Consider the color wheel. There are several different ways you can coordinate colors by looking at the color wheel. Complementary colors sit across from one another – think red and green – and they create the most dramatic looks. Analogous colors sit beside each other on the color wheel, and they create more subtle looks, allowing you to blend multiple colors.
- Pay attention to the tone and saturation of the colors you are using. You can combine several different colors and shades as long as your saturation levels – how deep the colors are – remain the same.

When it's time to start arranging the colors, start with the simplest patterns; alternating colors or using a simple A-A-B pattern can give you a good place to start. If you're using a lot of different colors and textures of beads, don't be afraid to use a random pattern either, grabbing whichever bead comes to hand quickest. While you may end up with a run of three of the same color in a row, the overall effect can be striking.

Materials and Things You'll Need

Beads and beading materials come in so many different forms, you may want to experiment with several to discover what type you like best. Not only do beads themselves vary tremendously in terms of color, pattern, size, shape, and material, but the materials you can use to thread them can also vary. Different types of beads also sit differently within a pattern, as well as move differently, while your different threading materials can also give you different end results even when using the same type and pattern of beads.

Therefore, it's important to consider your materials and how they will affect your end project before you begin.

Color and Bead Strings

While there are many specialty stores that sell beads individually, it's a lot easier – and cheaper – to purchase beads by the string. Many beads including glass, stone, ceramic, and metal will be sold strung together on a piece of nylon. Buying your beads this way is a nice way to see how the beads sit next to one another; round beads will sit very differently on a string than chips will, for example.

Some strings will also come with a variety of variegated colors mixed together. If you're unsure about putting colors together, this can be an easy route to take. Otherwise, consider laying out whole strings of beads beside one another in the store to start picking out the perfect colors for your design. Don't be afraid to select multiple beads of the same color as well, changing only things like texture or material to give your finished piece depth.

Irregular and Regular Beads

Beads come in multiple sizes and shapes as well as colors and materials. The biggest difference you'll notice, however, is in the beads' regularity. Stone bead chips, shell beads, and some glass beads will come in varying sizes and shapes within one group or strand. These irregular beads won't function the same way "regular" beads will, beads that have been machined to be uniform in size and shape.

Irregular beads can give you some very interesting looks, however, by giving you a randomness to the jewelry, even when using one bead or color. They can also be the perfect fit in some types of stitching or loom beading; an irregular bead may fit the corner or turn of a piece better than a round or oblong bead might.

Projects made with irregular beads tend to look a little more organic than those made with more uniform beads. So for those that prefer a more "natural" look, these beads might help you achieve the look you're after.

Wire

Many people prefer the use of thread, silk, or cord for beading, but you can get a lot of different looks by using wire. There are three basic types of wire: memory wire, which is difficult to shape, but retains that shape once you achieve it, standard wire which will bend more easily, but unbends easily as well, and woven wire, which acts like a cord, but with a metallic sheen. This type of wire works best for pieces where the thread is visible between the beads.

The key with working with wire is the gauge. Each gauge, or weight of the wire is assigned a number; the higher the number, the thinner and more pliable the wire. Look for 24 gauge wire for delicate wire wrapping or for creating multiple "strands" on a pair of earrings, or for 18 gauge wire to form a coil bracelet.

Jump Rings

Jump rings are fully formed circles of wire that are not easily unbent. You can join a bunch of them together to form a chain, hang several strands of beads off one ring, or use them as spacers between beads. You can usually find jump rings in two types: the first will require pliers to bend open and then shut again, while the second works more like a miniature key chain that you twist to attach to another.

Pliers

You will want at least two pairs of pliers when working

with beaded jewelry. One pair should have a flat nose, while the other should be rounded. Ideally, they should also be two different sizes to give you some more flexibility in this area. You'll need the pliers to hold small beads as you thread them, open jump rings, bend the end of a wire into a loop, or to close a crimp bead.

Beading Needle and Thread

If you plan on using actual thread for your beads, rather than cord or wire, you should invest in a beading needle as well. Beading needles are thin, flexible pieces of metal with a large eye. To use them, you tie the end of your piece of thread to the needle, then use the needle to string multiple beads at a time onto your thread. Most of the time, you'll use a beading needle with thin cotton or silk thread. This is ideal for coralling, stitching, or any type of beading where you want to double back through a bead or around the outside of a bead.

Making Your Own Beads

In addition to the beads that you can find in craft stores, bead stores, and specialty shops, there are also numerous types of beads that are easy to make yourself.

Making your own beads has a lot of advantages for jewelry makers:

- It's low cost, perfect for those who are on a budget, or who make a lot of jewelry
- It allows you to create unique and one of a kind pieces that may be unlike anything else that could be found in a store
- It gives you greater control over the project as whole; if you are unable to find beads that match your vision, you may be able to create those beads yourself to get the perfect finished look for your piece

Beads can be made out of nearly any material. Remember, that long before there were the types of mass-machined beads being sold today, that cultures and people where creating their own beads out a variety of different materials.

Wood Beads

Add a very lightweight, rustic, and often colorful touch to your jewelry with wooden beads. Making wooden beads is extremely simple, and can be done with objects you find in and around your home.

What you need:

- Several branches or sticks ranging in thickness from 1/8 inch to ½ inch
- Metal or wood trimmers
- Drill with a 1/16 inch bit

- Paint of your choosing

What to do:

1. Cut the branches or sticks into pieces ranging from ½ to 1 inch in length
2. Peel the bark from some of the pieces – you may want experiment with leaving the bark on some of your beads for additional texture
3. Drill vertically down the center of each piece of wood
4. Paint the exterior of the beads

Wooden beads are very light and easy to work with. You can mix them with other materials for a very unique and personal piece.

Shell Beads

If you live near the beach, you can make your own beads right out of the shells you find there. This technique works not only for small, whole shells but for those numerous tiny shell pieces that are often found all over the water's edge. Shell beads can add a lot of dimension, and mixed with things like glass and stone can make some beautiful vacation-style necklaces.

What you need:

- Shells or shell fragments of all sizes
- Diamond or carbide-tipped drill bit of about 1/16-inch in size
- Cooling oil
- Pliers
- Piece of wood block

What to do:

1. Grasp the piece of shell or shell fragment between the pliers.
2. Dip the end of the drill bit into the cooling oil.
3. Hold the piece of shell firmly against the wood block so the part you are drilling is in contact with the wood.
4. Set your drill to a high speed and drill quickly straight down through the shell until it reaches the wood belong.

[Excerpts from the first 3 Chapters]

CPSIA information can be obtained
at www.ICGtesting.com
Printed in the USA
LVHW080726060520
654932LV00009B/712